Contents

Note about the story

*Extremely Loud and **Incredibly*** Close* was written in 2005 and is Jonathan Safran Foer's second novel. Safran Foer is an American author who has lived in New York City for many years. This book is about a family in New York City and what happened to them after the attacks on the World Trade Center on September 11th 2001. The imagined story follows Oskar Schell, a clever nine-year-old boy whose father was killed in the attacks. Oskar is very sad about his father's sudden death, and he describes this feeling as having or wearing "heavy boots." We follow Oskar during his search for answers about how his father died and see how this young boy slowly and painfully returns to a more normal life.

*Definitions of words in **bold** can be found in the glossary on pages 93–96.

Before-reading questions

1 Look at the cover of the book. What do you think will happen in the story?

2 Read the "Note about the story" on page 4. The story happens in the city of New York. What do you know about New York? What is it like to live there, do you think?

3 Look at the title of the book. Oskar describes things as "extremely loud" or "incredibly close." What things in the story is Oskar describing, do you think? What do you think the title of the book tells you about the story?

4 Look at the contents page and the chapter titles. What do you know about the Empire State Building? Find out three things about this building. Why do you think Oskar goes there in the story?

5 Read the back cover of the book. Are these sentences *true* or *false*?
   a In the story, Oskar finds a key.
   b Oskar's father died a year before the World Trade Center attacks.
   c Oskar is looking for something in New York.

CHAPTER ONE
About me and my dad

Oskar Schell, September 2003

I like to **invent** things. For example, what if a **kettle** had a **spout** that opened and closed like a mouth, and it could sing or talk? Then our kettle could sing happy songs when it was making hot water. Or it could read a story in Dad's voice to help me fall asleep.

Another thing: there are lots of times when you need to escape quickly. But humans don't have their own wings, or not yet. So what about a very, very small **helicopter**? Or maybe a very small **parachute** with a motor. Then you would be able to fly away and be safe at any time.

I invent things to make myself feel better. Something else I do is to play my **tambourine**. For the last two years—since Dad died—I've had heavy boots. But playing the same sound again and again on my tambourine helps me, and makes me feel safe. One day, about a year after Dad died, I was playing it in my room when Ron came in and said he'd like to buy me a **drum set**. I really wanted a drum set, but I didn't want to say yes to him. He picked up my tambourine and started to shake it. I know he just wanted to be friendly, but it made me **incredibly** angry. "That's mine!" I told him, and I took it from him. What I really wanted to tell him was, "You're not my dad, and you never will be."

For my ninth birthday, which was last year, Grandma gave me a *National Geographic* magazine. She also bought me a white jacket (because I only wear white clothes), and she gave me Grandpa's camera. I asked, "Why didn't he take it with him when he left you?"

She said, "Maybe he wanted you to have it, Oskar."

I said, "But he left thirty years before I was born!"

Anyway, I read a really interesting thing in the magazine that Grandma gave me. It said that there are more people alive now than have died in all of human history. The number of dead people is getting bigger and bigger. So that gave me an idea. We should build **skyscrapers** for dead people that are built down, not up. They could be under the skyscrapers for living people that are built up. Then you could **bury** people 100 floors down, underground. There would be a dead world under the living world.

I also invented a new kind of skyscraper. It moves up and down while its elevator stays in the same place. If you want to go to the ninety-fifth floor, you just push the "95" button, and the ninety-fifth floor comes to you. It's extremely useful, and very safe. For example, imagine you're on the ninety-fifth floor and a plane **crashes** into a part of the building below you. The building will just take you quickly and easily to the ground.

On Sundays, Dad and I used to play a great game that was called "Search **Missions**." Sometimes the missions were quite easy, and sometimes they were extremely difficult. For the last mission, which never finished, he gave me a map of Central Park. "What are the **clues**?" I asked.

Dad said, "There aren't any clues. Not this time."

"Oh! Then what do I do?" I asked. He **shrugged** his shoulders, like he didn't know anything. I loved that.

I spent hours and hours walking around Central Park with Grandma, looking for clues. I took a photograph of every sign I saw. I read the information about each animal at the zoo. I decided to bring home everything I found to Dad: a coin, an old spoon, a pen, a pair of broken glasses. He was usually reading the *New York Times* at the kitchen table. He loved to read the newspaper and use a red pen to mark any mistakes he came across. Dad looked at everything I had found and said nothing.

I asked, "Have I found anything that's right?" Dad shrugged his shoulders again. He marked one more thing in the newspaper, then went to the bathroom. I looked at the page.

There was a sentence that said, "We will not stop looking for our daughter until we find her." There was a circle around "not stop looking." It wasn't a mistake! It was a message to me!

So I went back to the park for the next three nights. But the more I found, the less I understood. And then the Worst Day happened.

Tuesday September 11th 2001: the Worst Day

The night before the Worst Day, Dad put me to bed.

"Can you tell me a story?" I asked.

"Sure. If you promise not to ask lots of questions."

"OK. Of course!" I said.

The moment before he started a story was my favorite part. We were very close to each other, and I felt calm and quiet.

"Long ago, New York City had a sixth borough."

"Dad, what's a borough?"

"That's a question."

"I know. But I won't understand the story if I don't know what a borough is."

"It's a place where people live, like a **neighborhood**. Or lots of neighborhoods together," he explained.

"If there used to be a sixth borough, what are the five boroughs we know now?"

"Manhattan, where we live of course, then Brooklyn, Queens, Staten Island, and the Bronx. Anyway, the sixth borough was—"

"Dad, have I ever been—?"

He stared at me, then smiled. I stopped talking. He told

me the story of the sixth borough, and I listened carefully.

When he'd finished the story, he kissed my head, stood up, and left my room.

The next time I heard his voice was when I came home from school the following day, which was the Worst Day. We were let out of school early, because of what happened.

I look at my watch a lot, so I know that it was 10.18 a.m. when I got home. The apartment was empty and quiet. I walked to the kitchen and checked the phone messages.

Message One: Tuesday September 11th, 8.52 a.m.

*Hello? Is anybody there? It's Dad. If you're there, answer the phone. Listen, something's happened. I'm OK. They want us to stay in here and wait for the **firefighters**. I'll call later when I know more. I'm OK, so don't worry. I'll call again soon.*

There were four more messages from him.

Message Two: 9.12 a.m.

Message Three: 9.31 a.m.

Message Four: 9.46 a.m.

Message Five: 10.04 a.m.

I listened to them, and listened to them all again. Then, before I had time to think or feel, the phone started ringing.

It was 10.22.27 a.m.

I looked at the telephone number and saw that it was him.

I've only been in a **limousine** twice. The first time was two years ago, and it was terrible, because it was Dad's **funeral**. We were on our way to the **cemetery**. But I still loved the limousine. Mom let me sit next to the driver. I didn't want to sit in the back of the car with Mom and Grandma and think about the **coffin**—the empty coffin that didn't have my dad in it.

"What. Is. Your. Designation." I asked the driver.

"What?!" said the driver.

"He wants to know your name," Grandma said from the back seat. The man gave me his business card.

> **GERALD THOMPSON**
> Sunshine Limousine
> Across the five New York boroughs
> (212) 570-7249

"Hello. Gerald. I. Am. Oskar." I said.

"Why are you talking like that?" he asked.

"Oskar is a learning computer. He learns from contact with humans," I told him.

Gerald said, "O." and then he said "K." I wasn't sure if he liked me or not.

Mom was sitting in the back just staring out of the window. She looked very beautiful, but sad. It was difficult to talk to her after Dad died—she knew that I was closing the box of myself, and I knew that she didn't really love me.

CHAPTER TWO
How I met your mother

Thomas Schell

May 21st 1963, New York airport

A letter to my unborn child:

I want to tell you why I am now leaving New York, and leaving your mother. It's not an easy story to tell, but I will start by telling you how I met your mother.

*I haven't always been silent—I used to talk a lot. But, when I arrived in America from Dresden not long after the war finished, my words started disappearing. The first word I lost was "Anna." One day I tried to say, "That woman **reminds** me of . . ." But the word didn't come. I had loved Anna and had wanted to marry her. She was the only thing I wanted to talk about, but I couldn't say her name.*

*Then other words started to go, like leaves that fall from a tree into a river. I lost "come" one afternoon with the dogs in the park. Then I lost "want" and "hungry." After a time, I lost all of my words, and the **silence** was total. So I went to a **tattoo parlor**, and the man wrote "YES" on my left hand, and "NO" on my right hand. Now if someone asks me a question, I open my hands and show them these words.*

I started carrying a notebook with me, and I wrote the things I wanted to say in it—just one sentence on each page. At the end of each day I used to read through the pages of my life.

"Help me."

"I'm sorry—this is the smallest I've got."

"I'm not sure—it's late."

I often used all the pages before the end of the day. Sometimes I had to use some of the sentences in the notebook again. For example, someone might ask me, "How are you feeling?" I had to point at "I'm sorry—this is the smallest I've got" or "I'm not sure."

Then one day I met a woman in a café. She came over to me and said, "Are you Thomas? From Dresden?" I didn't answer her. She sat down next to me, and I saw that she was Anna's younger sister. I sat in silence as she talked about her day, her life. Then she said, "Don't you want to talk to me?" I found the next empty page in my notebook and wrote, "I don't speak. I'm sorry." We were both **lonely** and broken, and she started to cry. Then she wrote on the last page of my notebook: "Please marry me."

I turned the pages and pointed at "Ha ha ha!" She opened the book at "Please marry me." I pointed to "I'm not sure—it's late." She pointed again at "Please marry me." This time she pushed her finger on "Please."

I thought about the awful things that had happened to me during the war in Germany. I thought about my dead parents, and Anna. I thought about everything I had lost.

On the page where she had written "Please marry me," I wrote, "No children." That was our first **rule**.

"I understand," she told me.

The next day, your mother and I were married.

CHAPTER THREE
The year after my dad died

After Dad died, a lot of things frightened me, like tall buildings, planes, elevators, the subway, smoke, and strangers in the street. I was lonely and sad. It was worst at night, so I invented things to make myself calm.

Then something important happened. It was a year ago—so about a year after Dad had died. I was lying in bed, and I couldn't sleep. I'd invented about fifty things, but I still felt bad. Mom was in the living room, watching a movie with Ron and laughing. She wasn't sad, and she wasn't missing Dad. I got out of bed and went to Dad's closet. I touched his clothes. They smelled of him. I held his expensive watch, and I put my feet into his shoes. It made me feel a bit better.

I saw a blue **vase** on the top **shelf**. What?! I stood on a chair and put my foot on a shelf to reach higher. But I fell and the vase hit the floor and broke. I felt really, really bad. But Mom and Ron hadn't heard, and they didn't come.

Then I noticed a very small envelope in the middle of the pieces of glass. I opened it, and inside there was a key! It was smaller than our apartment key, but it looked important.

Next morning I told Mom I felt sick. I said I couldn't go to school. It was the first lie that I had to tell. Mom needed to go to work, so she sent me to bed to sleep. "Call Grandma if you need anything," she said.

When Mom had gone, I tried to put the key in all the locks in the apartment. It didn't fit any of them, so I knew that the lock must be outside of the apartment. But there are millions of locks in New York! I needed more clues.

I went to Walt's store, where Mom had got copies of our apartment key, and I showed Walt the key.

"Well, it's old. Perhaps twenty years old. It could be for a **safe-deposit box**, but I might be wrong," he said. "I think you should try the key in every lock you see." I put the key back in the envelope.

"Wait," said Walt. "Can I see the envelope?"

He looked at it very carefully and said, "Mmm, Black."

"What?" He was wrong. The key wasn't black, and neither was the envelope.

"It says 'Black,'" he said. He was right. The word "Black" was written on the envelope. How had I missed it?

"But why did Dad write a color on it?" I said, surprised.

"I don't think it's a color. It's a *name*," said Walt. "Because the 'B' is a capital letter, see?"

I looked on the internet. Black wasn't the name of a company that made safe-deposit boxes, or of a bank. That made my boots a bit heavy, so I did some other searches. Searches I shouldn't do. I made copies of the pictures I found: a lion attacking a girl, a soldier dying in Iraq, someone falling from the World Trade Center. I put the pictures in *Things That Happened to Me*, which is my **scrapbook** about my life.

The next day I told Mom I couldn't go to school again. That was the second lie I told. "What's wrong?" she asked.

"The same thing that's always wrong. I'm sad."

"About Dad?"

"About everything." I knew she had to go to work, but she sat down on the bed next to me.

"What's everything?" Mom asked.

I started counting on my fingers: "Car accidents, people without homes, eating animals, how the boys at school are horrible to me . . ."

Of course I wanted to talk to Mom about the key, but I couldn't. It felt like a secret between Dad and me. She put her hand on my leg, and we sat quietly for a few moments. "I understand," she said and gave me a **hug**. Then she went to work, and I stayed home.

When she had gone I looked on the internet again. I discovered that there were 472 people with the name Black in New York. But there were only 216 different addresses, because some of the Blacks lived together. I did some math. If I found four people called "Black" every weekend, it would take a year and a half to see all 472 of them.

I decided I was going to ask all the Blacks in New York about the key. And that was how the Lock Mission started.

I often think about the Worst Day—September 11th 2001. It was a year before the Lock Mission started. On that day I opened the apartment door and put down my **backpack**, like everything was wonderful. I didn't yet know that everything was actually horrible. I checked the phone. I listened to the five messages. I thought about running away. I thought about hurrying to the World Trade Center to see if I could save Dad myself. And then the phone rang. And it was him.

I knew I could never let Mom hear the messages, because my most important job is to look after her. So I took the money from Dad's desk—the money that he kept for emergencies. I went out to a store where I could buy exactly the same kind of phone as the one we had in the apartment. It was on a TV there that I saw that the first World Trade Center skyscraper had fallen. I ran home and recorded the answer machine message from the first phone on to the new phone.

Then I got a towel and put it around the old phone. Then I put that in a bag and put the bag in a box. Then I closed the box and put it under a lot of clothes in my closet. I didn't touch it again, not for months and months. Not until the night I decided to go on the Lock Mission, because then I really needed to hear his voice. So I got the old phone out and **plugged it in**.

Message Two: Tuesday September 11th, 9.12 a.m.

> *It's me again. Are you there? I hoped you would be. When you get this, call Grandma. Tell her . . . I'm OK. I'll call again in a few minutes. I think . . . the firefighters will be up here by then. I'll call.*

I used the towel, the bag, the box, and the clothes to hide the phone again. I quickly invented a few things. I held my tambourine very close to me.

I got out of bed, picked up the **walkie-talkie**, and went to look out of the window. I use walkie-talkies to talk to Grandma because she lives in the building across the street. I pushed the button and spoke. "Grandma? Grandma?"

"Oskar, it's very late. **Over**."

"Did I wake you up? Over."

"No. Over."

"Grandma, what were you doing? Over."

"I was talking to the **renter**. Over."

"But it's 4.12 a.m.! Over."

Mom told me not to ask questions about the renter. The renter had lived with Grandma since Dad died, but I still hadn't met him. That was strange, because I went there almost every day. He was always out, or sleeping, or in the shower. Or was Grandma imagining him?

"Oskar, what's wrong? Over."

"I miss Dad. Over."

"I miss him, too. Over."

"I miss him a LOT. Over."

"So do I. Over."

The phone messages made me sadder. But I couldn't explain that to Grandma, because they were a big secret. And the secret was a hole in the middle of me that every happy thing fell into.

"Did I ever tell you how Grandpa used to keep lots of different animals in the apartment? Over," Grandma said.

"Yeah, you told me a million times. Why did Grandpa leave? Over."

"He had to leave. But I don't know why. Over."

"Doesn't that make you angry? Over."

"No. Over."

"Sad? Over."

"Yes. Very. Over."

That night I put the key on a thin chain and wore it around my neck. I wanted to be close to it. I tried to invent something to keep the people you love near you at all times. I lay in the dark and thought for a very long time. But my head was empty. That made my boots incredibly heavy.

CHAPTER FOUR

Aaron Black and Abby Black

I decided to try to find all the people called "Black" in New York. I would start with A—"Aaron Black" and finish with Z—"Zyna Black." I wrote a list of all the Blacks and their addresses in my notebook. I bought a map of New York and used a red pen to mark where every Black lived. Then I packed a backpack with everything I needed: the map; the notebook; some small cards with my name, email address, and phone number on them; a **flashlight**; chocolate; juice; Grandpa's camera; and my tambourine. I made one rule about the Lock Mission: keep it a secret at home, but talk honestly about it to strangers.

On the first weekend I decided to visit the first two Blacks on my list. When I left the house I just said, "I'm going out. I'll be back later," and Mom didn't ask any questions.

It took me three hours and forty-one minutes to walk to Aaron Black in Queens, where I had never been before. I walked because I start to **panic** on buses, subways, and trains. I really don't like bridges, either. But sometimes you shouldn't think too much and should just do the thing you are frightened of. That's what Dad always used to tell me. So I took out my tambourine and shook it extremely loudly as I walked over the bridges.

Finally I arrived outside the right apartment building. I tried my key in the lock of the front door, but it didn't fit.

I found an apartment button that said "A. Black," and I pushed it. Nothing happened, so I waited, and then I pushed it again. Nothing. Then I pushed it and held my finger on it for fifteen seconds.

"All right, all right!" said a voice coming out of the wall.

"Hello," I said, nervously. "My name is Oskar Schell."

"What do you want?" He sounded mad.

"Did you know Thomas Schell?"

"No."

"Do you know anything about a key?"

"What do you want?"

"I found a key," I said, "and it was in an envelope with your name on it."

"Aaron Black?"

"No, just Black."

"There are a lot of people called Black. And it's a color."

"Yes, I know, but I really—"

"Goodbye."

"But—"

"Goodbye."

I sat down on the ground outside the building and started to cry. I wanted to scream and shout at everyone in the street. Instead I stood up and pushed the button again.

"What. Do. You. Want?" the man said.

"Thomas Schell was my dad."

"And?"

"*Was*. Not *is*. He's dead."

"Dead?"

"Yes. Dead. Gone. Not breathing."

There was silence for a few moments, and then he said, "How old was he?"

"He was forty."

"That's too young." There was more silence, and then he said, "Can I ask how he died?" I didn't want to talk about it, but I remembered my rule, and so I told him everything. When I'd finished he said, "If you come up here I'll have a look at the key for you."

"I can't come up. You're on the ninth floor, and I don't go up that high."

"Oh. Well, I can't come down to you. I'm very sick—that's why it took me a long time to answer when you called."

I didn't know what to do, so I ran away. I heard him saying, "Hello? Hello? Please!" as I turned away. If I could do it again, I would do it differently. But I can't do it again.

Abby Black lived in a house in Greenwich Village. It took me two hours and twenty-three minutes to walk there from Aaron Black's neighborhood. By the time I arrived my hand was very tired from shaking the tambourine. I tried the key in the door, but again it didn't fit, so I knocked loudly and waited.

A woman opened the door and said, "Can I help you?" She was incredibly beautiful, and her face looked like Mum's face.

"Hi," I said.

"Hello."

"Are you Abby Black?"

"Yes."

"I'm Oskar Schell."

"Hello."

"Did you know Thomas Schell?" I asked.

"Excuse me?"

"Did you know Thomas Schell?" I repeated. She thought for a few moments.

"No."

"Are you sure?"

"Yes." But she didn't sound very sure. Was she keeping a secret from me? So I showed her the envelope with "Black" written on it.

"Does this mean anything to you?" I said.

"I don't think so. No . . . it doesn't," she said, but I didn't believe her.

"Would it be OK if I came in?"

"Listen, I really don't think I can help you."

"I'm really thirsty," I said, thinking quickly.

"There's a café on the opposite side of the road."

"Actually, I don't feel very well. I need a drink straight away." It was a lie, and I know it's very bad to lie, but I really needed to spend more time with her.

She stared at me for a moment, and I heard a man's voice calling something from inside the house. Then she said, "Follow me," and turned and walked into the house. Everything inside was clean and tidy, and there were beautiful big photographs on the walls. When she was getting me a cup of coffee the man in the other room called again, this time extremely loudly. He seemed **upset**, but Abby didn't seem to notice him. "I love that photo," I said, pointing to a picture of an elephant's head that was on the wall in the kitchen.

"Thank you," she said.

I got incredibly close to the photo, and I could see a **tear** running down the elephant's cheek. "It's an amazing photo, but it's not really correct," I said.

"What do you mean?"

"Well, elephants can't cry. Humans are the only animals that can cry."

"Oh," she said and looked very carefully at the picture.

"I think someone used a computer to add the tear," I explained.

"I read somewhere that elephants are the only other animal to bury the dead bodies of other elephants," she told me.

"No," I said, "that's wrong. They just push the bones together in one place. Only humans bury their dead."

Abby was silent.

"May I take a photo of it for my scrapbook?"

She nodded, so I pulled Grandpa's camera out of my backpack and took the photo. After I had put the camera back, I noticed that she was crying. I didn't know why she was crying, so I didn't know what to say. Was she crying about the elephants? Or the upset person in the other room? Or something else I didn't know about?

Suddenly the kitchen door opened, and a man walked into the room. He looked angry and said something I didn't understand, and then he walked away again. Abby didn't look at him or say anything.

"Who was that?" I asked.

"My husband," she answered.

"Does he need something?"

"I don't care."

"But he's your husband, and I think he needs something." That made her cry more. I walked over to her and put my hand on her shoulder, like Dad used to do with me.

"You must think this is all very strange," she said.

"I think most things are strange," I told her.

"How old are you?" I told her I was twelve, which was another lie. I wanted to be old enough to be important to her. "What's a twelve-year-old doing knocking on the door of a stranger?"

"I'm trying to find a lock," I told her. "Are you *sure* you didn't know Thomas Schell?"

"No, I didn't know him." I don't know why, but I *still* didn't believe her. I pulled the key out from under my shirt, because it was still on the chain that was around my neck.

"And what about this key? Have you seen it before?" I said, and I put it in her hand. The key was on the chain, so when she moved forward to look at it her face came incredibly close to mine. We sat like that for what seemed like a long time, not speaking. I didn't want to move.

"I'm sorry," she said at last. "I don't know anything about the key."

"I'm sorry, too."

"Can I take a picture of you?" I asked when I had put the key back under my shirt. She seemed surprised, but she let me take the photo. She didn't want me to take a picture of her face, so I took a photograph of the back of her head.

When I left I gave her one of the cards with my name and email address on it. "In case you remember anything about the key, or just want to talk," I told her.

CHAPTER FIVE
Why I am leaving New York

May 21st 1963, New York airport

*I've been writing this letter to you in the airport. I used to come here to pick up the magazines that travelers left here. Your mother loved to read them and learn new English words. During the week I used to work in the **jewelry** store, and then every Friday I came here to get the magazines. I often took an empty **suitcase** with me and brought it back full of all kinds of different magazines, and your mother used to read them all. I loved coming to the airport—I used to sit here for hours and watch people meeting each other. I watched them running into each other's arms, full of excitement and love. I liked the kissing and the crying, and the end of missing someone. It filled my heart with happiness to see it all, but the happiness wasn't mine—it was theirs.*

Maybe that's what I was hoping for when I met your mother. I hoped we could come together, save each other, and make each other happy. It didn't work. Instead we have shared our lives for many years but have continued to be sad and lonely.

*Since very early in our **marriage** we have had lots of rules. We never talk about the past; we never listen to sad music; I am not allowed to watch her cook; she is not allowed to watch me write; and the animals we keep in the apartment are all mine, and only I can feed them. There are many more rules, but most of them are very strange, and I can't explain them.*

The rules made us more unhappy, and they made life very difficult. The most impossible rule of all was "No children." And, because she really needed you, she broke that rule. At first she kept you secret, but in the end I had to know.

Today I am at the airport with terrible **sadness** in my heart. I am leaving your mother and returning to Germany. I think she knew that I was going when I left the apartment this morning, but she didn't stop me. I am sitting here writing in my notebook, and I have much more to tell you, but the book is filling up. There aren't enough pages for all the things I need to say. I'm sorry. That is what I've been trying to tell you. I'm sorry for everything. I'm sorry that I loved Anna — her sister — more than I loved your mother. I'm sorry that I didn't save Anna from the bombs in Dresden. I'm sorry for what I am now doing to your mother, and to you. I'm sorry I will never be able to see your face, feed you, and tell you bedtime stories. You will want to know why I left. But how can I possibly explain it? I can't carry on here. I've tried, and I can't. The sadness is too great. You probably won't understand. Your mother might not even give you this letter. I will take these pages out of the notebook and post them to her, in an envelope addressed to "My Unborn Child," before I get on the plane. I am gone. I am no longer here.

With love,
Your father — Thomas Schell

CHAPTER SIX
About my grandma

Grandma always looked after me when Mom and Dad were at work. We spent a lot of time playing and learning. She stayed at our apartment during the week after Dad died, while Mom was going around Manhattan putting up pictures of Dad. We watched TV together, made cakes, and went for lots of long walks in the park.

One day, while she was looking at something in the park, I hid from her. I liked the way it felt to have someone looking for me, calling my name: "Oskar! Oskar!" Well, I don't think that I *liked* it—I *needed* it at that moment.

I followed her without her seeing me, and I saw her begin to panic. She was crying and running around, shouting my name again and again. I still didn't tell her where I was, because I knew that she would laugh a lot later, when she found out it was a **joke**.

I watched her as she started to walk home, knowing that she had lost me, probably **forever**. I ran a different way and got to the apartment building before her. Then I hid behind the front door and jumped out the moment she arrived. I laughed and laughed. But she didn't laugh. Instead she stared hard at me and started to say something, then she stopped. She turned around and silently went across the street to her apartment. Later, when I looked across the street, I saw something on her window. I used my **binoculars** to see what it was, and it was a note that said in big letters, "Don't go away."

We didn't talk about it, but, since that day, when we go on walks she makes us play a game. She calls my name every few minutes, and I have to call back and say, "I'm OK!"

We've spent a lot of time together over the years, especially since Dad died. She tells the same stories about Grandpa again and again, and I tell her about my **inventions** and the boys at school who are horrible to me. But I never told her about the Lock Mission.

When I got home after visiting the first two Blacks on the first day of the Lock Mission, I went over to Grandma's apartment. That's what I did every Saturday afternoon, while Mom was working. I walked up the seventy-two steps and rang the **doorbell**. She didn't answer, which was unusual. So I opened the door, because she always leaves it unlocked, which probably isn't safe.

As I walked in I saw her coming toward the door. I thought her eyes looked a bit red. "Oskar!" she said, and she lifted me off the ground with a huge hug.

"What were you doing?" I asked.

"I was in the other room, talking to the renter. What about you? What have you been doing?"

I didn't tell her about the Lock Mission, or about any of the other things that happened between that day and a year later, when I **dug up** Dad's empty coffin. I don't know why I didn't tell her. It gives me incredibly heavy boots now to think that I didn't.

The next weekend I continued the Lock Mission. I followed my rule and kept the Mission a secret from Mom. I used to tell her, "I'm going out. I'll be back later." But she never asked me any questions. That was really strange because usually she worried about me a lot. Had she fallen in love with Ron and started to forget about me? When I left our apartment to go searching for the lock, I became a little lighter, because I was getting closer to Dad. But I also became a little heavier because I wasn't close to Mom.

The next person I went to see was Abe Black in Coney Island. I'm good at walking, but I knew I couldn't walk that far, so I used some of my birthday money to take a cab.

Abe Black was friendly. He wanted me to go on a **roller coaster** with him, but, of course, I'm incredibly **panicky** about roller coasters. "It would be really sad to die without riding on my favorite roller coaster," he told me. In the end I agreed. We sat in the first car, and we went down as fast as a rocket. I felt the wind against my face. It was fun, but it was also sad. It made me think about the people who had jumped from the World Trade Center before it fell down. Had they felt the wind in their faces like this?

I enjoyed meeting Abe. It was almost a wonderful day, except that Abe didn't know anything about the key or Dad. At the end of my time with him he said, "Hey, I have to drive to Manhattan now, so do you want a ride with me?"

"I don't get in cars with strangers, and how did you know I was going to Manhattan?" I said.

"I'm not a stranger, and I don't know how I knew."

CHAPTER SEVEN
Mr. Black

This might be hard to believe, but the next Black lived in our apartment building, just one floor above us. But, strangely, I'd never seen him. I walked up to his apartment and tried my key in the lock. It didn't fit, so I knocked loudly on the door. After an incredibly long time the door opened. "Hello! Can I help you?" a very old man asked extremely loudly.

"Yes, hello. I live downstairs. May I please ask you a few questions?" I said.

He turned to walk back into the apartment. I guessed that I was supposed to follow him, so I did.

We went into the kitchen and sat down at the table. Then he just started to talk, still extremely loudly.

"Well, I've had an amazing life!" he told me. I thought that was strange, because I hadn't asked him any questions yet.

"I was born on January 1st 1900! I lived every day of the twentieth century!"

He told me that he had lived through both World Wars and that he had been a journalist—his job had been to write about wars. His wife hadn't liked that. He was very interesting, and we talked for a long time. Then I took out the key and asked him about it.

"No, I don't know what that key opens!" he shouted.

"Did you know my dad, Thomas Schell? He lived on the floor below you," I said.

"No, I don't know that name!"

"Are you 100% sure?" I asked.

"I've lived long enough to know that I'm not 100% anything!"

I decided that I really liked him.

"Where is your wife?" I asked him.

"Oh, she died twenty-four years ago! But it feels like yesterday!"

"Oops," I said. "I'm sorry I asked about her."

"No, don't be sorry! Thinking about her is all I have now! I haven't left this apartment since she died!"

"What? You haven't been outside for twenty-four years?" I said. I couldn't believe it.

"That's right! My feet haven't touched the ground! I just call for food, and they bring it to me! I order my clothes and pens over the phone!"

"But you used to travel so much," I told him. "Don't you miss the world?"

"I do! Very much!" he replied.

My boots were very, very heavy now. This lonely man had been right near me, all my life, and I hadn't known. I hadn't been able to help him. We sat there in silence for a few moments.

Then, suddenly, I thought of something—something enormous and wonderful.

"Do you want to help me to find the lock?" I asked.

"You're really clever, and you know a lot. And it would be great to have a friend who's an adult with me. Please say yes."

He looked at me, then closed his eyes and became quiet. I wasn't sure if he was thinking about the idea, or thinking about something else, or if he was asleep. After a while I said, "Mr. Black?" Nothing.

I touched his arm, and he looked up suddenly.

"Oh! I couldn't hear you! I was looking at your mouth earlier and guessing what you were saying!" he said. "I turned these off a long, long time ago!" He was pointing to his **hearing aids**, which I hadn't noticed before.

"Shall I turn them on for you?" I asked him. He looked at me and smiled a little. I walked behind him and looked carefully at the hearing aids.

"Do it very, very slowly!" he said. There was a very small wheel on the back of each one, and I turned each one slowly and carefully. Then I sat down opposite him. We looked at each other.

Then, suddenly, lots of birds flew by the window, extremely fast and incredibly close. There were about twenty of them. Mr. Black immediately put his hands over his ears and started to cry.

"Mr. Black, are you OK?" I whispered, very gently. The sound of my voice made him cry more, and he nodded his head to say yes. He stood up and walked around the room, listening carefully to anything that made a noise.

I wanted to stay there watching him listen to the world, but it was late. I told him I would come to his apartment the next Saturday at 7 a.m. "We'll start the next part of the mission then," I told him.

My boots were incredibly heavy after I met Mr. Black. When Mom put me to bed later that night I told her, "Mom, please promise that you won't bury me when I die."

She sat next to me and put her hand on my cheek. "You're not going to die any time soon. You have a long, long life ahead of you."

"But I can't spend forever in an extremely small box underground."

"Don't you want to be buried next to me and Dad?"

"What? But Dad isn't even there!"

"But his **memory** is there."

"No, it's not! It's just a stupid empty box!" I told her. "Oskar . . ."

"His body isn't there!"

"Don't talk like that."

I was really angry now. "Why not? It's true!"

"Oskar! Stop saying these things."

"No!" I shouted. "And don't lie to me."

"Lie to you? About what?"

"Where were you?"

"Where was I *when*?"

"On the day Dad died."

"I was at work," she told me.

"Why didn't you pick me up from school like all the other moms? Why weren't you here when I got home?" I shouted, angrily.

"I got home as soon as I could. I wanted to be here, but it wasn't possible."

"I don't care."

Mom didn't say anything. She just started to cry.

I slowly moved closer to her and put my head on her shoulder. "I miss Dad," I said.

"So do I," she told me.

"Do you really?"

Mom said, "Of course I do. How could you ask that?"

"But I hear you laughing," I said, "when you're in the living room . . . with Ron."

"I do laugh every now and then, but that doesn't mean I've forgotten Dad. I cry a lot, too," she said, quietly.

"I don't see you cry."

"I try not to cry in front of you. Oskar, I'm trying to find ways to feel happy again."

"Are you in love with Ron?" I asked her.

"Ron is a great person," she said. Why do adults often give you an answer to a question you haven't asked? I stared at her, and she said, "He's my *friend*. He's having a difficult time, too, and we help each other."

"Promise me that you won't fall in love."

"Why would you ask me to promise that?"

"Either promise me that you'll never fall in love again, or I'm going to stop loving you," I told her.

"Oskar, you're not being fair."

"I don't have to be fair! I'm your son!"

She let out an enormous breath and said, "You remind me a lot of your father."

"I want Dad to be here now!" I told her. And then I said something very, very bad. I didn't know I was going to say it, and it was something nobody should ever say: "Why can't *you* be dead instead?"

She looked at me for a second, then stood up and walked out of the room. I wanted her to shout at me, but she didn't. She walked out and then closed the door gently, like she always did. I could hear that she didn't walk away.

"Mom?" I heard nothing. I got up and went to the door. "I take it back."

"You can't take something like that back," I heard through the door.

That made me feel very, very sad. I lay on the hard floor for a long time, and then I took out the old phone. I needed to hear Dad's voice.

Message Three: Tuesday September 11th, 9.31 a.m.

Hello? Hello? Hello?

CHAPTER EIGHT
More Blacks

I really wasn't enjoying school. The kids there were horrible to me, and everyone thought I was strange. So I liked the Lock Mission because every weekend I had a plan and something to do. And now I wasn't doing it alone—I was doing it with Mr. Black.

At 7 a.m. the next Saturday I went to pick up Mr. Black from his apartment. "So, where are we going, Oskar?" he asked.

"The Bronx," I said.

"OK. It's a long time since I've been on a subway train!" he said.

"I never use trains, subways, buses, or boats. They're too dangerous. We're going to walk," I told him.

"Walk? But it's about twenty miles from here," he said. "I'm too old to walk that far." He was right. It was hard to imagine him walking to the end of our street.

Most of the subway journey was underground, which made me very panicky, but I closed my eyes and was brave. When we got off the train and started to look for the right street, Mr. Black took my hand. I think he was frightened because the neighborhood looked really poor and dangerous. It wasn't long until we found the right address for Agnes Black, who lived on the second floor of an apartment building. There wasn't an elevator (which I was pleased about), so Mr. Black waited at the bottom of the stairs while I walked up.

I rang the doorbell and waited. A small woman in a **wheelchair** opened the door, and I said, "Excuse me, are you Agnes Black?"

She said, "No speak English!"

"What's your name?" I asked her.

"*No entiendo!*"

I turned and shouted down the stairs to Mr. Black, "She doesn't speak English!"

"Well, what does she speak?" Mr. Black asked.

"I think it might be Spanish."

"That's great! I speak a bit of Spanish!" he told me.

I pushed her wheelchair to the top of the stairs, and Mr. Black and the woman shouted to each other. They seemed to talk a lot, and laughed a little, too. Then Mr. Black shouted up to me again, "Oskar! Come down now!"

When I got back to the ground floor, Mr. Black told me what she had said. Agnes Black was gone. She had been a waitress at Windows on the World.

"What!" I said. "That was the restaurant at the World Trade Center. My dad had a meeting there the day he died. Maybe she knew my dad, or gave him coffee or something."

"It's possible," said Mr. Black, and he put his arm round me. "Let's go and see the next Black."

I shook my tambourine as we walked to the subway, holding my breath when we went back underground.

Albert Black came from Montana. He wanted to be an actor, but he didn't seem to have acted in anything important. He didn't know about the key.

Alice Black was incredibly nervous because she lived in a factory building that people weren't supposed to live in. Before she opened the door, she shouted, "Promise me that you aren't the police!"

"Why don't you look at us through that very small hole in the door?" I said.

So she did, and then she said, "Oh, it's you," which I thought was really strange. She opened the door, and we followed her into a big, open space. There were drawings of the same man all over the walls and on the tables, too.

"Did you draw all of these?" I asked her.

"Yes." I didn't ask her who the man was. If you draw someone that much then you must love them and miss them very much. I did ask her about the key, but she didn't know anything about it.

Allen Black's job was to stand on the front door of a building on Central Park South, and that's where we found him. He said he hated being a doorman because it was boring. He showed us a very small TV that he kept in his pocket that played movies. Allen didn't know anything about my dad or the key, so we said goodbye.

"Good luck, Oskar," he said as we were leaving.

"How did you know my name was Oskar?" I asked.

Mr. Black said, "Because you told him."

"Did I? I don't remember," I said.

Arnold Black didn't say very much at all. He opened the door and immediately said, "Sorry, I can't help you."

"But I haven't told you what I need help with yet!" I said.

He started to cry a bit, and then he just said, "I'm sorry," and closed the door.

Mr. Black said, "Oh, well! Let's go to the next one!" I nodded, and I privately thought that Arnold Black was very strange.

When I got home I had dinner with Mom, and then I went to my room. I started to think about Agnes Black again. Maybe she and Dad had died together. Maybe they were talking to each other until the building fell. Or maybe they had gone up to the roof together. In my scrapbook I had copies of photos that showed people holding hands and jumping from high up on the building. So maybe they did that. I would never know.

I took the box out of the closet, and the bag out of the box, and the towel off the phone.

Message Four: Tuesday September 11th, 9.46 a.m.

> It's Dad. It's Thomas Schell. Hello? Can you hear me? Are you there? Pick up. Please! Pick up. I'm underneath a table. Hello? Sorry. I have a wet towel against my face. Hello? No. Try the other. Hello? Sorry. People are panicking a bit. They want us to go up on to the roof. The helicopters are trying to get close enough to take people off. Please pick up. I don't know. Yeah, that one. Are you there?

Why didn't he say goodbye? Why didn't he say he loved me?

CHAPTER NINE
My story

December 4th 1978, Germany

To my child:

I am writing this to you from Dresden. I want you to know that, although you haven't received any letters from me, that doesn't mean I haven't written any. Every day I write a letter to you. I want to tell you what I experienced, all those years ago, here in Dresden. If I could tell you about it, maybe I could forget it all and come home to you. I don't think that's possible, but I want to try.

*One evening in February 1945, Anna and I were talking, and I told her how much I loved her. The war was terrible, but people said that it would be finished soon. She and I talked about where we would live after the war, and we planned to have children together. That evening was the last time I ever saw her. As I walked home I heard the planes coming—there were 100 of them flying over Dresden in the dark. When I saw them coming toward me I knew that something awful was about to happen. I ran down the stairs of our **cellar** as fast as I could, but before I had time to say anything there came the horrible, frightening sound of bombs. My family and I were thrown to the ground, and the cellar filled with fire and smoke. It seemed like the world was going to end.*

When it stopped we came out of the cellar, and we didn't recognize anything. There was fire everywhere we looked, and all that was left of our house was the front wall with the front door in it.

"I have to find Anna!" I told my mother.

"Don't go!" my father said. "You mustn't go!" But I needed to find Anna. I told my parents I would come back and meet them at our front door. I reached out and touched the **doorknob**. I felt pain and pulled my hand quickly away and then touched it with my other hand, too. I don't know why I did that. When I looked at my hands they were badly burned—they were red, and the skin had gone. My father shouted at me. It was the first time he had ever shouted at me, and I can't write here what he said. Then, although he had never hit me before, he hit me hard across the face. That was the last time I saw my parents.

On my way to Anna's house the second group of planes came, and the bombs began to fall again. I hid in another cellar, and, when that was bombed, I ran through the streets again. Dead and dying people were lying on the floor, and I stepped on them in my panic. I saw so many horrible things, but the worst was a young woman on fire. She was running toward me with a silent baby in her arms, and her eyes were searching for help—help that it was impossible for me to give. The memory of that baby and the awful pain on the woman's face will always stay with me.

I kept running, and my hands kept **bleeding**. All I could think about was that silent baby. I went past the zoo and saw animals running around, frightened and badly hurt. One of the zoo keepers saw me and caught me by the arm. "Do you know how to shoot?" he asked. He pushed a big gun into my hands and shouted, "You have to find the **carnivores**!"

I said, "I don't know which animals are the carnivores."

He told me, "Then shoot them all, shoot everything!"

I don't know how many animals I killed, but it was a lot. I shot an elephant that was lying on the ground and screaming. I killed a monkey that was sitting on a wall, staring at me and pulling its own hair. There were two lions that were standing quietly beside each other, and I shot them both. Were they brother and sister? Friends? Lovers? Can lions love?

When the bombing finally stopped I ran to a river by a bridge and fell down. I pushed my burning, bleeding hands into the cold water. I was in a lot of pain, and my hair had been burned off. I was later told that soldiers came and took more than 220 bodies away from that bridge. Four of the bodies came back to life as the soldiers were moving them, and I was one of them. I was in a hospital for hours, or days, or weeks— I don't know how long it was. When I finally left the hospital I searched for my parents and for Anna, but I never found them. I believed they were dead, but I never knew for sure.

When I met your mother I wanted to explain everything, about Anna, and the bombings, and the silent baby. I wanted to tell her that I was too afraid of losing someone I loved to love anyone again. But I couldn't speak. It was all locked inside me. So here I am, thousands of miles away from you and her, writing another letter that I may not be able to send.

I love you.
Your father

CHAPTER TEN
The Sixth Borough

My memory of that last night I spent with Dad is very clear, when he told me that last bedtime story.

"Long ago, New York City had a sixth borough," he had started. "The Sixth Borough was an island, with just a thin bit of water between it and Manhattan. And some people—the people who were really good at sport—could jump across the water to the island if they tried really hard. Everyone loved that—the crowds used to clap and cheer every time someone managed to jump from Manhattan to the Sixth Borough."

"It sounds fun!" I said.

"Yes, it was. But every year, fewer people could make the jump. Soon only one or two people could do it. At first everyone thought the jumpers were eating too much and getting too fat to jump. But it wasn't that. It was because the Sixth Borough was moving."

"Moving?"

"Yes, just a millimeter at a time, but it was moving away from New York. A few years later, no one could jump across at all. And then the eight bridges between Manhattan and the Sixth Borough started to break away, one at a time, and fall into the water. The phone lines broke, too, which meant that people had to shout, or they had to write letters. They made the letters into paper planes, and they threw them across the water to the other side."

"Didn't people try to stop the island moving?" I asked.

"Yes, of course. They called the engineers, who tried everything to stop it going. They even used chains to try to pull it back, but nothing worked. It was incredibly sad because some people had friends and family over there, and they were moving slowly but surely away. But, of course, there was also Central Park to think of."

"What do you mean?" I asked.

"Well, Central Park used to be right in the center of the Sixth Borough. It was the best and most beautiful part of the borough. But, when everyone realized that the Sixth Borough was definitely going and couldn't be stopped, the engineers decided to save the park."

"How?"

"They put enormous **hooks** deep into the grass of the park. Then the park was pulled by the people of New York, like a **rug** across a floor, from the Sixth Borough into Manhattan.

"All the children of New York were allowed to lie down on the grass as it was moved. They lay on their backs next to each other, filling every part of the park. Bands played wonderful music, and there were beautiful **fireworks**, which disappeared in the air just before they reached the ground. And then the children were pulled, one millimeter and one second at a time, into Manhattan. By the time the park stopped moving, every child had fallen asleep, and the park was full of their dreams."

"Dad?"

"Yes?"

"Was there really a sixth borough?"

He looked at me and smiled. "Well, you can choose if you believe it or not. You just have to look at all the clues, and then decide for yourself."

"What clues?"

"Well, there are lots of them. For example, if you walk twenty-four steps directly east from the gate into the play park, there is a tree. If you look on that tree, you will see two names cut into it. But there's no **record** of those names in the phone books, or in hospital records, or anywhere. Actually, they have studied all the names on all the trees in Central Park, and 5% of them aren't listed in any records."

"That's really interesting," I said.

"But because all of the Sixth Borough's documents were lost when the Sixth Borough moved away, we will never be sure. Some people believe they are made-up names. Others believe they belong to people who were lost forever on the island, which slowly moved away to Antarctica."

"What do you believe?" I asked him.

"Well, it's hard for anyone to spend more than a few minutes in Central Park without feeling that they're experiencing something special. Or that there's some magic there, right?"

"I suppose," I said.

"Maybe we're just missing things we've lost, or hoping

for what we want to come. Or maybe it's the memory of the children's dreams from that night the park was moved."

Dad stopped talking, and there was silence as I thought about everything he had said.

"That was an amazing story, Dad."

"I'm pleased that you think so."

"Dad?"

"Yeah?"

"I just thought of something. Perhaps some of those things I dug up in Central Park were actually from the Sixth Borough."

He shrugged his shoulders, which I loved. Then he kissed my head, stood up, and left my room.

CHAPTER ELEVEN
The Empire State Building

Mr. Black and I spent months looking for the lock together. The last person we visited was Ruth Black, and the address for her was the eighty-sixth floor of the Empire State Building. That was strange because I didn't think people lived there.

I felt panicky about going up so high and having to use the elevator, but Mr. Black said it was OK to feel that. He patiently encouraged me to do it.

"OK, OK," I said after a long time. "I'll come with you."

In the elevator I held Mr. Black's hand and was incredibly nervous. When the elevator door opened, we were on the floor where tourists can look out at the city below. I knew it should be an exciting place to be, but I couldn't stop imagining a plane flying toward the building and crashing into it. I stood still and imagined what the last second would be like. There would be an extremely loud noise, and it would feel like the building was going to fall over. I know that is what it felt like from all the descriptions I've read on the internet. Then there would be lots of smoke and people screaming all around me. It would get so hot that my skin would start to burn. Then I would have to choose if I stayed there and burned, or jumped into the street, where it was cool, but I would definitely die. Which would I choose? Would I jump, or would I burn? And there would still be a few seconds to call someone on my cell phone. Who should I call? What should I say? I didn't know.

I stopped myself thinking those thoughts and started to look around. Mr. Black was very near the edge and was looking at Central Park. Near him was an old woman who was holding a **clipboard**. She stared at me as I walked toward Mr. Black. It made me feel uncomfortable, and even Mr. Black noticed it.

"You know what," he whispered. "I think she's the one." For some reason, I knew he was right. But, before we had decided which of us should go and talk to her, she had come to us.

"Hello! I'm Ruth. Shall I show you around this very special building?" she said.

Mr. Black said, "Yes, please! We'd love to know more."

So she started showing us around and telling us all about the history of the building. She read us a lot of information and numbers from her clipboard, but we laughed a bit, too, and Mr. Black asked questions. Half an hour later, at the end, Mr. Black said, "That was wonderful, thank you."

She said, "You're very welcome. I really, really love this building."

Mr. Black smiled. "You're a great lady," he said. "Would you like to have tea with me one afternoon?" I hadn't known that Mr. Black wanted a girlfriend.

"I'm sorry." she said. "I can't, because I stay up here."

Mr. Black said, "What? Always?"

"Yes," she said.

"But how long have you been up here?" Mr. Black asked.

"For many years," she said. I asked her where she slept. "On nice nights I sleep out here," she told us. "But, when it gets cold, I have a bed in one of the small rooms inside the building."

"What do you eat?" I asked.

"Oh, there are two small cafés up here. And sometimes people bring me food," she said.

"But why are you here? Why don't you ever go down?" Mr. Black asked.

"My husband used to go around the city selling things," she told us. "One day he found an old **spotlight**. It was a really bright light, so he fixed it to the **cart** that he used to push around the city. He told me to come up to this floor of the Empire State Building. As he walked around New York, every now and then he used to shine the light up at me so I could see where he was."

"Did it work?" Mr. Black asked.

"Not during the day—I looked, but I couldn't see it in the daylight. But in the late afternoon, when it started to get dark, it was amazing. I remember that first night. I came up here, and everyone was looking all over, pointing at the things to see. But I was the only person who had something pointing back at me."

"Or someone," I said.

"Yes!" she said. "I felt like a queen. And when the light went off, I knew he had finished work, and I used to go down and meet him at home. When he died, I came back up here. I just didn't want to go home, because he wasn't there. I know it's crazy."

"No," I said. "It isn't."

"It reminded me of looking for his light in the daytime," she said. "I knew it was there, but I just couldn't see it."

Mr. Black took a step toward her. "I wouldn't make you go down," he said. "We could spend the afternoon together up here."

"I'm not very good with people," she said.

"Neither am I," Mr. Black said.

"I don't even have a nice dress," Ruth said.

"Nor do I," said Mr. Black. It was a good joke, and Ruth laughed. But then she put her hand over her mouth, like she was angry at herself for forgetting her sadness.

I really didn't want to go in the elevator again. So I had to walk the 1,860 stairs down to the ground floor, while Mr. Black went in the elevator and waited at the bottom for me. We were both really tired, so we decided to go home. But, when I took Mr. Black to his apartment, he said to me, "Oskar, I think I'm finished."

"Finished with what?" I asked.

"I've loved being with you. I've loved every second of it," he told me. "You got me back into the world, and that's the greatest thing anyone has ever done for me. But now I think I'm finished. I hope you understand." He reached his arm toward me, waiting for me to shake his hand.

I kicked his door and told him, "You're breaking your promise."

I pushed him and shouted, "It isn't fair!"

Then I said a really bad word.

No, I didn't do that. Instead I shook his hand and walked away. I didn't know what to do. I was all alone again, and I still hadn't found the lock.

CHAPTER TWELVE
Alone and not alone

When Mr. Black told me he was finished, my boots were the heaviest they had ever been in my life. I couldn't talk to Mom, so I decided that I needed to talk to Grandma.

I ran up the seventy-two stairs to her apartment and rang the doorbell. She didn't answer, so I rang again and waited. Then I opened the door and went in.

"Grandma? Hello?"

I thought maybe she had gone to the store, or perhaps for a walk in the park, so I sat on the sofa and waited. I was very worried about her and invented terrible accidents that had happened to her. I got a bit panicky and started looking around the apartment for her.

"Grandma?"

I looked everywhere—in the dining room, the kitchen, the bathroom, and in Grandma's bedroom. In the bedroom I opened the top **drawer**, where I thought her clothes would be. I don't know why I did that. It was filled with hundreds of envelopes, carefully put in rows. I opened the next two drawers down, and they were also filled with envelopes.

I pulled out one envelope from each drawer. They all had the same writing on them, and they had been mailed from Dresden in Germany, which is where Grandma came from. I went through all the envelopes and checked the date stamps on them. There was one for every day, from

May 31st 1963 to the Worst Day. Some were addressed "To my unborn child." Some were addressed "To my child." What?!

I knew I shouldn't do it, because they didn't belong to me, but I opened one of the envelopes. It was sent on February 6th 1972. It was empty. I opened another, from another drawer, with the date November 22nd 1986. It was also empty. June 14th 1963—empty. They were all empty. But where were all the letters?

I heard a sound from the guest room. I panicked a bit and quickly closed the drawers. I thought for a moment. It must be the renter. He was real!

The door of the guest room was closed, but when I got down on my knees I saw that the light in the room was on.

"Grandma?" I whispered. "Are you in there?"

There was no reply. "Is someone in there?" I said more loudly. "I'm looking for my grandma because I really, really need her."

After what seemed like a long time, the doorknob slowly turned. The door opened, and I saw a very old man.

"Are you the renter?"

He showed me his left hand, which had YES **tattooed** on it. Then he turned and went back into the room. When he came back, he was holding a little notebook. He opened it at the first page and wrote, "I don't speak. I'm sorry."

"Who are you?" I asked.

He turned to the next page and wrote, "My name is Thomas."

"That was my dad's name," I told him, "but there are lots of people called Thomas. He died."

On the next page he wrote, "I'm sorry."

We stood there. I didn't know what to say to him, and he didn't know what to write to me.

I told him, "I'm Oskar. My grandma isn't here, is she?"

He showed me his right hand, which had NO on it. He wrote, "She went out."

"Where?" I asked. He shrugged his shoulders, just like Dad used to.

"If you want to come in," he wrote, "we could wait for her together." I went into the room with him and sat down on a chair.

"How long have you been living here?" I asked.

He wrote, "What has your grandmother told you?"

"Well," I said, "since Dad died, I think, so nearly two years." He opened his left hand.

"What's your story?" I asked.

He thought for a moment, then shrugged his shoulders and wrote, "I don't know."

"Where were you born?" He shrugged his shoulders.

"You don't know where you were born!" He shrugged his shoulders. "Where did you grow up?" He shrugged his shoulders. This man didn't seem to know anything. He was a bit strange, but because Grandma wasn't there, and I really needed to talk, I said, "Can I tell you my story?"

He opened his left hand.

So I told him how I had broken the vase and found the key, and the envelope with "Black" on it. I told him about the voice of Aaron Black, and how beautiful Abby Black was, and how I had put her photo in *Things That Happened to Me*, my scrapbook. I told him about Abe Black and the roller coaster, and Agnes Black, who was dead. Then there was Alice Black, with all her drawings, and Allen Black the doorman with his very small TV. I told him about all the other Blacks I had met, too, because now I had visited all the Blacks up to the letter "R," including Ruth.

Finally, I told him all about Mr. Black and how he had told me he didn't want to continue with the Mission. "And now I don't know what to do," I told the renter. "I haven't found the lock, and I don't know anything that I didn't know when I started my search. I've had to tell lots of really bad lies. And the worst thing is that I miss my dad more now than when I started. I wanted to do the Lock Mission so I could *stop* missing him." All the time I was speaking, the renter was looking at me and listening carefully.

I told him, "It hurts too much."

He wrote, "What does?"

Then I did something that surprised even me. I ran down the seventy-two stairs, across the street, and up the 105 stairs to my apartment. I went to my room and got the old phone. Then I ran back to Grandma's apartment. The renter was sitting on the same chair, in the same way, like I'd never left. I took the phone out of my backpack and plugged it in. I played the five messages and then pushed the "Stop" button.

"No one has ever heard those messages except me," I said.

He looked very serious, and worried or upset, I wasn't sure. Finally, he wrote, "Why was he in the World Trade Center?"

"He was there for a meeting. He went there quite a lot," I told him.

"What kind of meeting was it?" he wrote.

"He runs the family jewelry business, which my grandpa started."

"Who's your grandpa?"

"I don't know. He left my grandma before I was born. She told me he really liked animals and used to keep lots of them at home. She says that he could talk to them."

"What do you think about your grandpa?"

"I don't think about him," I said.

He pushed the "Play" button on the phone and listened to the messages again. Again I pushed "Stop" after the fifth message finished.

Message Five: Tuesday September 11th, 10.04 a.m.

> It's . . . it's . . . Dad. Hello . . . so . . . Dad. . . . know if . . . hear any . . . this . . . I'm . . . Hello? . . . you hear me? We . . . to the roof . . . everything . . . OK . . . fine . . . sorry . . . hear me . . . much . . . happens, remember . . .

We sat in silence for a while, and then I said, "I need to know how he died."

"Why?" he wrote.

"So I can stop inventing how he died," I told him. "I found videos on the internet of bodies falling from the World Trade Center. When I look very closely at the videos, there's one body that could be him. It's dressed like he was, and I think it might be wearing glasses, like him. It probably isn't him. But I want to believe that it's him."

"You want him to have jumped?"

"I want to stop inventing. If I knew how he died, I wouldn't have to invent him dying inside an elevator, for example. That actually happened to some people. Some people in the Windows on the World restaurant tried to use **tablecloths** like parachutes—sometimes I imagine Dad doing that. There were so many different ways to die, and I just need to know which was his."

The renter held out his hands like he wanted me to take them. "Are those **tattoos**?" I asked him. He closed his right hand.

"Why don't you talk?" I asked.

He wrote, "I can't."

"When was the last time you talked?"

He wrote, "A long, long time ago."

I asked, "Can I take a picture of your hands?" I wanted to put it in my scrapbook.

He put his hands on his knees, open, like the pages of a book. YES and NO.

I took Grandpa's camera out of my backpack, and I took the photo, and then I went home.

CHAPTER THIRTEEN
Everything becomes clear

I really wanted to fall asleep that night, but I was too upset.

I invented lots of small strange things, and then a thought came into my head that wasn't like the other thoughts. It was closer to me, and louder. I didn't know where it came from, or what it meant, or if I loved it or hated it: what about digging up Dad's empty coffin?

So the next day I went back to see the renter to ask for his help.

Over the next few weeks he and I met in secret and started to plan how we would dig up Dad's coffin. During those weeks I also continued the Lock Mission without Mr. Black, and I visited maybe thirteen or fourteen other Blacks. But the mission wasn't the same— I didn't feel like I was getting closer to Dad, and I'm not sure I believed in the lock any more.

When I got home after visiting Peter Black, after eight months of searching around New York, I was tired and sad. Mom and Ron were in the living room watching TV. I went to the kitchen to get some ice cream, and I saw the phone—the new phone. I hated it and hadn't touched it or even looked at it since the Worst Day. There was a small red light on it, so I pushed the "Play" button.

Hi, this is a message for Oskar Schell. Oskar, this is Abby Black. You were just at my apartment asking about the key. I wasn't totally honest with you, and I think I might be able to help. Please give—

The message just stopped after "Please give—." Abby Black was the second Black I had visited, at the very start of the Lock Mission. Her message had been there for eight months.

I packed my backpack and went into the living room.

"Mom?" I said.

"Yes?"

"I'm going out. I'm not sure when I'll be back, but it could be late."

"OK," she said. Why didn't she ask me where? Why didn't she try to stop me?

It was beginning to get dark, so I was a bit nervous, but I got the subway to Abby Black's house. When I got there the front door was open a little, like she knew I was coming. But of course she couldn't know that, so why was the door open?

"Hello? Is anyone there? It's Oskar Schell," I called.

She came to the door. "Hello, Oskar!" she said. "I thought you weren't going to call me back. It's been months since I left that message."

We went inside the house, and we talked. "I told you I didn't know anything about the key," she said. "But, actually, my husband knows something."

"Why didn't you tell me when I came?" I asked.

"I couldn't, because I'd just had a terrible fight with my husband."

"But it was about my dad, who is dead!"

"I didn't tell you because I wanted to hurt my husband."

"Why?"

"Because he had hurt me."

"Why?"

"Because that's what people do," she told me.

"I spent almost a year searching because of you!"

"But I called you months ago, just after you left."

"You hurt me!" I shouted, angrily.

"I'm very sorry," she said.

I was still angry, and I started to cry. She **hugged** me, and I started to calm down. But then suddenly, from nowhere, a thought came to me, and I moved away from her.

"Why did the message you left stop in the middle of a sentence?" I asked.

"Oh, that must be when your mom picked up the phone."

"You spoke to my mom?"

"Yes, for a few minutes."

"Did you tell her I came here?" I asked. "Did you tell her about the key?"

"Well, I thought she knew, so yes, I think we talked about all that."

I couldn't believe it. None of it **made sense**. Why hadn't Mom said anything? Or done anything? And then the answer came to me. I suddenly understood why

Mom never asked me where I was going when I went out. She didn't have to, because she knew. Maybe she had even seen my map and notebook.

Now it made sense that Abe knew that I lived in Manhattan, and Alice had said, "Oh, it's you." Then Allen the doorman had said, "Good luck, Oskar," when I was sure I hadn't told him my name. They all knew I was coming. Mom had talked to them all before I went to see them.

I thought about Mr. Black. He probably knew that I was going to knock on his door that day. Mom probably told him to look after me, to go around New York with me to keep me safe. Did he even really like me? Were his amazing stories even true? Were his hearing aids real?

Did Grandma know?

Did the renter know? Was the renter even the renter?

I saw now that the Lock Mission was a theater play that my mom had written. And she already knew the ending when I was at the beginning.

To check all of this I asked Abby, "Was your front door open because you knew I was coming?"

She didn't say anything for a few seconds, and then she said, "Yes."

"Where is your husband?" I asked.

"He's my ex-husband—we're not married now. He's probably at work."

CHAPTER FOURTEEN
William Black

Abby took me to her ex-husband's office, which had "William Black" written on the door. I knocked on the door, and a voice said, "Come in."

William Black had gray-brown hair, a short beard, and round glasses. From behind his desk he asked, "What can I do for you tonight?"

"Did you know my dad, Thomas Schell?" I asked. He thought for a minute, then said, "No, I don't know any Schells."

"You said 'know,' not 'knew.' My dad is dead, so you couldn't know him now."

"Oh, I'm sorry to hear that."

"But maybe you did know him. I found a little envelope that had your name on it. At first I thought it was your wife's name, so I spoke to her. But she was really sad and said she didn't know anything about it. And your name is William, so I hadn't reached Blacks with names starting with 'W' yet."

"So what was so special about the envelope?" he asked.

I pulled out the key on the chain around my neck and showed it to him. "It said 'Black' on the envelope, and this was inside it."

He said, "I can't believe it! I've spent two years looking for this key."

"And I've spent a year looking for the lock."

I was finally able to ask the most important question of my life. "What does the key open?"

"It opens a safe-deposit box."

"Was it my dad's?" I asked.

"Your dad's?" He sounded surprised.

"Yes. I found the key in my dad's closet. I couldn't ask him what it meant, because he's dead, so I had to find out myself."

"Did you find it in a blue glass vase?"

"Yes!"

William Black started to explain. "A couple of years ago my father became very ill. The doctor told him he would only live for two more months. Because he knew he was going to die, he started writing lots of letters. He wrote to everyone he knew, to say goodbye and to tell them anything important he wanted to say."

"Did he write one to you?" I asked.

"Yes. But I couldn't read it for a few weeks."

"Why not? Didn't you want to know what it said?"

"It was too painful. You see, my father and I weren't very close. I didn't want to keep any of his things, so in those first few weeks after he died, I decided to sell them all."

I thought that was bit strange, because Dad's things were all I wanted, but I didn't say anything.

"I had a street sale, and people I didn't know came and bought everything—even his sunglasses and his wedding suit. It was a terrible day, maybe the worst day of my life." He stopped speaking for a moment, then went on. "Anyway, that evening, after the sale, I opened the letter and read it. I was hoping he would say that he loved me, or that he was sorry. But there was none of that. It was just a short letter that explained things I needed to know—where he kept his important documents and what he wanted me to take care of."

"Did that make you sad?" I asked.

"I was angry. But I'm not any more."

I told him I was sorry, and then I asked him about the key.

"At the end of the letter my father wrote, 'I have something for you. In the blue vase, on the shelf in the bedroom, is a key for a safe-deposit box at our bank. I hope you'll understand why I wanted you to have it.'"

"What was in the safe-deposit box?" I asked.

"But that's the problem," he said. "I didn't read the letter until after I had sold all of his things. I had sold the vase to your father, so the key had gone."

"What?! You met my dad?"

"Yes, just once."

"Do you remember him?"

"A bit. He was a nice man. He said he was buying the vase as a gift for his wife for their wedding **anniversary**."

"That's on September 14th!" I said.

"I went to the bank and told them what had happened. But they said that, without the key, they couldn't help me. So I tried to find your dad, but I didn't know anything about him, not even his name. I made a few signs with pictures of him and put them on street lamps. But this was the week after the September 11th attacks, so there were hundreds of signs about people everywhere."

"My mom put signs up about him, too."

"What do you mean?"

"He died in the September 11th attacks."

"What! I'm so sorry. I didn't realize."

"It's OK." We both sat in silence for a moment, thinking.

"Well," I said. "At least you've now found what you've been looking for."

He said, "I'm so sorry. I know you've been looking for something, too, and this isn't what you needed to find."

"That's OK," I said, but I started to cry.

"Are you all right?" he asked, kindly.

"Can I tell you something that I've never told anyone else?"

"Of course."

"On that day, they let us out of school early. I didn't really know what had happened, but I knew it was something bad. My mom and dad were both working, so I walked home. When I got home I saw a little red light on the phone, so I listened to the messages. There were five, and they were all from him."

"Who?"

"My dad," I said.

William looked shocked and put his hand over his mouth.

"He just kept saying that he was OK, and that everything was going to be fine, and that we shouldn't worry."

A tear went down William's cheek and on to his finger.

"But this is the thing I've never told anyone," I said. "After I listened to the messages, the phone rang. It was 10.22 a.m. I looked at the phone, and I saw that the number was Dad's cell phone."

"Oh, no . . ."

"Please could you sit beside me so I can finish what I need to say?"

"Of course," he said, and he moved his chair from behind the desk so he could sit next to me.

"I couldn't pick up the phone. I just couldn't do it. It rang and rang, and I couldn't move. And then the answer machine came on, and I heard Dad's voice: 'Are you there? Are you there? Are you there?'

"He needed me, but I couldn't answer. 'Are you there?' he asked, not 'Is anyone there?', so I think he knew I was in the apartment. He asked eleven times. There are fifteen seconds between the third and the fourth time, like he was giving me time to be brave and answer. You can hear people screaming and crying, and glass breaking. That's why I think maybe people were jumping. The phone cut off after the fifteenth time. That sixth message is one minute and twenty-seven seconds long. So it ended at 10.24 a.m., which is when the building fell down."

"I'm so sorry," William said, and then he gave me a really big hug.

I asked him, "Do you forgive me?"

"For not being able to answer the phone?" he asked.

"For not being able to tell anyone about it," I said.

"Yes," he said. "I do."

I carefully took the chain with the key off my neck and put it over his head. It was then that I knew I was ready to dig up Dad's coffin.

CHAPTER FIFTEEN
The second time I lost you

September 11th 2003, Manhattan

To my child:

I wrote my last letter in Dresden on the day you died, and I thought I'd never write another word to you. But here I am, sitting in New York in the same apartment I lived in years ago, and I want to tell you what has happened.

It was two years ago today that I lost everything for the second time. I had just finished writing a letter to you, and I was walking in the street in Dresden when I saw a crowd of people in front of a shop. I stopped to see what they were looking at. And it was there, on many different TVs in the shop window, that I first saw the plane crash into the World Trade Center.

The TVs repeated the video again and again. In the days that followed, I read the lists in the newspapers of the people who had died: grandfather of fourteen, chef, new mother, Yankees fan, nurse, window washer, sister, bird watcher . . . And then one day I saw it: "Thomas Schell. He leaves behind a wife and son." I stared at the page and thought about my son, and my grandson. I knew I needed to do something. I put all the letters I had ever written to you into suitcases, and I got on a plane to New York.

I didn't know if your mother would want to see me. So I wrote a note addressed to her and gave it to the doorman of your mother's apartment building. The note said, "I'm sorry." Then I waited across the street. I saw your mother get out of a big black limousine and go into her apartment building with a small boy. Forty years had passed, and she had changed a lot, but I still knew her. Later I saw the boy come out and go into a building across the street. Nothing happened for the rest of the day. I wrote another message that said, "Do you want to see me again, or should I go away?"

The next day I saw a note on her window that said, "Don't go away." I still didn't know what to do. So I gave another note to the doorman that said, "Do you want to see me again?" I waited and waited, but no more messages appeared on her window. I went to ask the doorman if there was a note for me. There wasn't, but the doorman gave me a key. I went up in the elevator and saw that the apartment door was open. So I put the key safely in my pocket and walked in. She called to me from another room, "Only the guest room!" That was how we slowly began our strange second life together.

Every afternoon someone used to come to the apartment. I could hear the door opening, and I could hear a child speaking and playing. One evening, when your mother came and left food outside my room, I asked her, "Is that my grandson?"

She replied, "No, he's my grandson."

"Can I meet him?"

"No. Because I taught him how to speak. I cried when he cried. I held him when he couldn't sleep. When he was angry, it was me that he shouted at."

But she agreed to let me see him. The next day I got into the coat closet and waited, so that I could see him through the keyhole. When the doorbell rang, she opened the door, and I saw his white shoes. "Oskar!" she said, hugging him close.

"I'm OK!" he replied. In his voice I heard my own voice, and my father's and grandfather's voices. So that must be your voice, too—it was like hearing your voice for the first time.

I wanted to talk to him, but I didn't know what I would say. "I'm sorry"? "I love you"? Maybe I needed to tell him all the things I couldn't tell you, or give him all the letters that were supposed to be for you. But I knew that your mother definitely wouldn't let me do that.

I thought about how I could be close to Oskar and still be fair to your mother, and fair to you, and fair to myself. I started to watch him and learn about his life. I followed him to school; I watched him walk around the city; I discovered which stores he liked to look in. I thought I could go on like that forever, but I was wrong. After a while some of the things he was doing seemed strange. He was going out on his own a lot, and visiting strange places. I was the only one watching him, and I was worried that his mother let him go so far alone. Then every weekend he started leaving his apartment building with an old man, and they went knocking on doors all around the city. I made a map of where they went, but I couldn't understand what they were doing. Who was the old man? Why did they only spend a few minutes at each apartment? Were they selling something, or getting information? After they left one house I waited and

then knocked on the door. "I can't believe it!" the woman
said. "Another visitor!"

"I'm sorry," I wrote. "I don't speak. I'm his grandfather.
Why was he here?"

She said, "About the key—he was looking for the lock."

"What lock?"

"Don't you know?" the woman said. I didn't know.

For months I followed him and talked to the people he
talked to. I was trying to learn about him while he was trying
to learn about you. All of this really **upset** me. Why can't we
all just say what we mean at the time?

One day, Oskar and the old man went up the Empire State
Building. I waited on the street outside for more than an
hour before I saw the old man come out of the elevator. He
was alone, so I started to worry about Oskar. Had this man
left Oskar up there all alone? I hated him. I started to write
something in my notebook, but he came up to me and held
me by the arm. "I don't know who you are, but I've seen you
following us. Go away!"

"I'm Oskar's grandfather. I don't speak. I'm sorry," I wrote in
my notebook and showed him.

"Oskar doesn't have a grandfather," the old man said.

I wrote as quickly as I could and explained everything. After
he had read my words he said, "Oskar wouldn't lie to me."

"He didn't lie. He doesn't know," I wrote.

"If it's true, then you are the person who should be going
around New York with him, not me."

"I have been," I told him. "But without him knowing."

We heard Oskar singing. He was about to walk around the corner—his voice was getting louder. The old man said, "He's a good boy," and then he turned and walked away.

I went straight home and sat on my bed. I thought about packing my things and leaving, or jumping out of a window. Someone rang the doorbell, but I didn't get up or answer it. I didn't care who it was. I wanted to be alone. But then the person came in and called, "Grandma?" It was him, Oskar. I didn't know what to say, or what to do. And then he just told me everything—the vase, the key, Coney Island, the Bronx, the Empire State Building, and Mr. Black. The poor child, telling everything to a stranger. I wanted to build walls around him and save him. He talked and talked, and I could see that he was full of terrible sadness. "My dad, my dad," he said, and then he ran to his apartment and brought me a phone. I heard your last words.

The last message ended suddenly. You sounded very calm—you didn't sound like someone who was about to die. There is so much that I want to tell you and to write about. But I have no more pages in this notebook.

When Oskar left the apartment, I told him to come when his grandmother was out if he ever needed me. The very next day he came to me and said, "I want to dig up Dad's coffin."

We talked for weeks about how we would do it. And then one day Oskar told me he was ready. We would do it on the second anniversary of your death.

Your father

CHAPTER SIXTEEN
Hope returns

After I met William Black, I met with the renter to make our last plans for digging up the coffin. There was one thing that neither of us had talked about until that day. Then the renter said it. "What will we do when we've dug the coffin up and opened it?" he wrote in his notebook.

I told him, "We'll fill it." We talked about what we could put in it—Dad's clothes, or his red pens, or the old phone that made me feel guilty. But nothing seemed right.

Then the renter wrote, "I know. I have an idea. I'll tell you tomorrow."

The next evening I put everything I needed in my backpack and then went into the kitchen to have dinner. Mom had made spaghetti, and Ron ate with us. I asked him if he still wanted to buy me a drum set, because I had decided I would like one. He said yes. Then I asked him why he didn't have his own family.

Mom said, "Oskar!"

"It's OK," said Ron, and he put down his knife and fork. "I did have a family, Oskar. I had a wife and a daughter, but they were killed in a car accident."

"Oh," I said. "I didn't know that."

"Your mom and I met in a group for people that have lost family. That's where we became friends," said Ron. I didn't look at Mom, and she didn't look at me.

I hadn't known that Mom was in the group.

"Why didn't you die in the accident?" I asked.

"I wasn't in the car," Ron said.

"Why weren't you in the car?" I asked.

Ron looked down at his plate and said, "I don't know."

"It's strange that I've never seen you cry," I said.

He said, "I cry all the time, but in private."

After that I said I was tired, and Mom put me to bed. It was 9.36 p.m. when she left my room. I lay there in bed, with my eyes wide open, waiting for 11.50 p.m. When that time came, I got up very carefully, took my backpack from under the bed, and left the apartment as quietly as I could. The renter was waiting for me under the street lamp. He had a **shovel** and two suitcases with him. I didn't ask him what was in the suitcases, because I thought it was better to wait until he told me. At 12.00, Gerald arrived in the limousine, and I thanked him for coming on time. He opened the door for us, and we got in. It was my second time ever in a limousine.

At 12.56 a.m. we stopped on the road outside the cemetery, and Gerald agreed to wait for us there. I put on my backpack, and the renter took the shovel and suitcases, and then we climbed over the wall into the cemetery. It was very dark. We had to use my flashlight to read the writing on all the stones to find the right one. We found the place where Dad's coffin was buried at 1.22 a.m. and started to dig. It was much harder than I had imagined, and it took a long time to move all the earth. I called Gerald's cell phone and asked him to come and help us. It was 2.56 a.m. when we found the coffin and cleaned the earth off it. Gerald went back to the limousine and left us on our own. When I opened the coffin, I was shocked at how empty it looked. The renter opened the two suitcases, and I saw that they were filled with papers. I asked him what they were.

"I lost a son," he wrote.

"How did he die?"

"I lost him before he died," he told me.

"How?"

"I went away because I was afraid of losing him."

I wasn't sure what he meant, so I asked him, "What are all those papers?"

"They are letters I wrote him—things I wasn't able to tell him."

To be honest, I don't know what I understood then. I don't think I guessed that he was my grandpa. I didn't think that the letters in the suitcases might be something to do with the empty envelopes in Grandma's bedroom. But I think I understood something, because it seemed right to put the letters in the coffin, which is what we did.

When I got home, it was 4.22 a.m. and Mom was on the sofa. I thought she would be incredibly angry with me, but she just kissed my head.

"Don't you want to know where I was?" I asked.

"I trust you," she said. "You would tell me if you wanted me to know."

"Are you mad at me?"

"No."

"Is Ron mad at me?"

"No."

"Are you sure?"

"Yes." I started to cry a bit, and then I put my arms around her and hugged her.

"I promise I'm going to be better soon."

"There's nothing wrong with you."

"I'll be happy and normal. I tried incredibly hard. I did my best."

She said, "I know. If Dad were here, he'd be very proud of you."

"Do you think so?"

"I know he would."

I wanted to tell her everything, about all the lies I'd told her, about the phone. I wanted her to tell me it was all OK.

She said, "Dad called me from the building that day."

"What? On your cell phone?" She nodded yes, and it was the first time I'd seen her letting all her tears run out.

"What did he say?"

"He told me he was on the street, that he'd escaped from

the building. He said he was walking home."

"But he wasn't."

"No."

"Did he make it up so that you wouldn't worry?"
I asked.

"Yes, he did."

"But he knew that you knew it wasn't true."

"Yes." I put my arms around her and pushed my head
into her neck. We both cried a lot. She was my mom, and
I was her son, and that was the most important thing in
the world.

I told her, "It's OK if you fall in love again."

She kissed me and said, "I won't fall in love again."

I told her, "I want you to."

She said, "I love you."

After that I went to my room and got into bed. My
hands were still dirty, but I wanted them to be dirty.
I wanted the memory of that night to be on them. I picked
up *Things That Happened to Me* from next to my bed. There
were no more empty pages in the scrapbook—it was
totally full. I had read somewhere that it was the paper
that kept the World Trade Center burning for so long—all
of the notebooks, printed emails, and photographs of the
workers' children. Maybe if we didn't have so much paper,
the world would be a safer place. Perhaps I shouldn't start
another scrapbook. I opened the book and looked through
the maps of New York, lists of the Blacks I had visited, the
things I had photographed with Grandpa's camera, and

pictures from the internet. I saw the photo of the man falling from the World Trade Center. Was it Dad? Maybe.

I slowly turned the book around until the man looked like he was flying upward toward the window and the sky, not falling down toward the ground. What would it be like if everything that had happened could happen backward? If that was my dad, he would now fly back into the window and leave the messages on the phone backward. The plane would fly backward out of the hole in the skyscraper and return safely to Boston. Dad would go backward all the way back to our apartment that morning. He'd go back to bed and dream backward, get out of bed and put his clothes on, then walk backward into my bedroom. Then he would sit on my bed very close to me and tell the story of the Sixth Borough backward. We would be close to each other, and we would be safe.

During-reading questions

Write the answers to these questions in your notebook.

CHAPTER ONE

1 What things does Oskar invent? Why does he invent them?
2 Oskar calls one day "the Worst Day." Why?

CHAPTER TWO

1 When and where is the letter written?
2 Who might be writing this letter?
3 The two people in this chapter decide to marry each other. How did they know each other in the past?

CHAPTER THREE

1 What does Oskar find, and where does he find it?
2 What is written on the small envelope, and what does it mean?
3 On "the Worst Day," why does Oskar go to a shop to buy a new phone?

CHAPTER FOUR

1 What things frighten Oskar?
2 Why can't Oskar meet and talk to Aaron Black face to face?

CHAPTER FIVE

1 Who is Thomas Schell writing this letter to?
2 Why does Thomas Schell say, "I am at the airport with terrible sadness in my heart."?

CHAPTER SIX

1 Why does Oskar hide?
2 Why is Grandma so upset when she can't find Oskar?
3 Who is Ron?

CHAPTER SEVEN

1 Who is Mr. Black? Describe him.
2 What good idea does Oskar have about Mr. Black?

CHAPTER EIGHT

1 What has happened to Agnes Black?
2 Why is Agnes Black important to Oskar?
3 Why does Oskar shake his tambourine?

CHAPTER NINE

1 Which time and place does the letter describe?
2 How does what happened in 1945 in Dresden change Thomas?

CHAPTER TEN

1 In the story that Oskar's father tells, what happens to "the Sixth Borough"?
2 In the story, what happens to Central Park and why?
3 What do you think the main message of the Sixth Borough story is?

CHAPTER ELEVEN

1 Who is Ruth Black, and where does she live?
2 In what ways are Ruth Black and Mr. Black similar?
3 Why does Oskar think, "I was all alone again."?

CHAPTER TWELVE

1 What does Oskar find in Grandma's bedroom?
2 "What do you think about your grandpa?" the renter asks. Why do you think he asks this?

CHAPTER THIRTEEN

1 Who is the phone message from, and when was the message left?
2 Oskar says, "And then the answer came to me." What was the question, and what is the answer?

CHAPTER FOURTEEN

1 Why does William Black say, "I can't believe it!"?
2 When and why did William Black meet Oskar's father?
3 What does Oskar tell William that he hasn't told anyone else?

CHAPTER FIFTEEN

1 What does Thomas Schell mean when he says, "I lost everything for the second time."?
2 Thomas asks, "Is that my grandson?" and Grandma tells him, "No, he's my grandson." What does she mean?

CHAPTER SIXTEEN

1 What do we learn about Ron?
2 What do Thomas and Oskar put in the empty coffin?
3 What new information does Oskar's mother give Oskar?

After-reading questions

1 Look at your answers to the "Before-reading questions." Were you right?
2 Describe Oskar. How does he change during the novel?
3 Why do you think Oskar's grandfather sent hundreds of empty envelopes to New York, but kept all the letters with him in Germany?
4 Does *Extremely Loud and Incredibly Close* have a happy ending, do you think? Why/Why not?

Exercises

1 Match the words with the definitions in your notebook.

Example: 1—*e*

1	bury	**a**	complete quiet, no sound
2	crash	**b**	a long box that a dead person is put into
3	funeral	**c**	to hit something hard and suddenly
4	cemetery	**d**	an event that is about a dead person
5	coffin	**e**	to put something or somebody in the ground
6	silence	**f**	unhappy because you are alone
7	lonely	**g**	a place where we bury dead people

CHAPTER THREE

2 Put the sentences in the correct order in your notebook.

a .... The World Trade Center skyscraper fell, and Oskar's father died.

b .... The renter started living at Grandma's apartment.

c ....*1*.... Oskar came home from school and listened to five messages.

d .... Oskar copied the answer-phone message on to the new phone.

e .... Oskar decided to start the Lock Mission.

f .... A year passed after Oskar's father died.

g .... Oskar found a key in a blue vase.

CHAPTER FIVE

3 Write the correct answers in your notebook.

1 Thomas Schell ***used to love*** / **was loving** going to the airport to pick up magazines for his wife.

2 Thomas **would have hoped** / **hoped** that he and his wife **would be** / **are** happy together.

3 **Since / By** very early in their marriage they **have / have had** lots of rules.

4 Thomas believes he **will never be able to / can never be able to** see his son's face.

5 Thomas **is trying / has been trying** to tell his son that he is sorry **for / since** years.

6 The letters to his son **might not ever arrive / can't never arrive** in New York.

CHAPTERS SIX AND SEVEN

4 **Complete these sentences in your notebook, using the words or phrases from the box.**

| joke | inventions | roller coaster | hearing aids |
| dig up | doorbell | binoculars | memory | journalist |

Oskar wanted to play a ¹............*joke*............... on Grandma, so he hid in the park. After that, Grandma went home and put a note in her window. Oskar used his ²............ to read it. He then went to visit her, and he rang the ³............ When she answered she looked upset. He didn't tell her about his ⁴............, the Lock Mission, or the plan to ⁵............ his father's coffin. Next he went to see Abe Black, and he decided to go on a ⁶............ After that he went upstairs in his apartment building to visit Mr. Black. Mr. Black was a very old man and wore ⁷............ But he still had a very good ⁸............ and told Oskar about when he used to be a ⁹............ .

5 **Complete these sentences in your notebook, using the words or phrases from the box.**

can't	can	doesn't have to	shouldn't	had to

1 Oskar is sad that he ....*can't*.... talk to his mom about the Lock Mission.

2 Oskar knows that he .... touch the envelopes in Grandma's bedroom, but he opens some of them.

3 "............ I tell you my story?" Oskar asks the renter.

4 Oskar .... tell a lot of lies to people when he was on the mission.

5 Oskar .... tell the renter all his secrets, but he decides to.

CHAPTERS THIRTEEN AND FOURTEEN

6 **Write the correct names in your notebook.**

Mr. Black	Mom	Abby Black	Oskar
	William Black	the renter	

1 ....*Mr. Black*...... has stopped coming on the Lock Mission.

2 .... has had an idea and makes a new plan.

3 .... has agreed to help Oskar with his new plan.

4 .... has been waiting for Oskar to come and visit her again.

5 .... has been watching Oskar and talking to all the people he visits.

6 .... has been looking for a key for two years.

CHAPTER FIFTEEN

7 **What happens here? Match in your notebook.**

Example: 1—b

1 Grandpa reads about his son's death
2 Grandpa hears Oskar's voice for the first time
3 Grandpa sees Oskar
4 Grandpa meets Mr. Black
5 Grandpa meets Oskar for the first time

a in Grandma's apartment.
b in Dresden, Germany.
c through a keyhole.
d outside the Empire State Building.
e from Grandma's guest room.

Project work

1 Imagine you are Oskar's mother. Write a diary entry about the day you found out about the Lock Mission.

2 Oskar's father tells a story about the Sixth Borough. Write a short story or poem about what happened to the people who lived there after the borough moved away to Antarctica.

3 In Chapter Fifteen, Grandpa says, "Why can't we all just say what we mean at the time?" Write about the reasons why the different characters in the book often don't say what they are really thinking.

4 How do Oskar and Grandpa change after the story, do you think? Write reasons for your answers.

An answer key for all questions and exercises can be found at **www.penguinreaders.co.uk**

Glossary

anniversary (n.)
a day that is one, two, three, etc. years after something important happened

backpack (n.)
a bag that you wear on your back

binoculars (n.)
You use *binoculars* to see a very long way. They are made of two round parts that you hold against your eyes.

bleed (v.)
If a part of your body is *bleeding*, blood is coming out of it.

bury (v.)
to put a dead body under the ground

carnivore (n.)
a person or animal that eats meat

cart (n.)
A *cart* has two wheels. You put things in it and push it along.

cellar (n.)
a room under a building

cemetery (n.)
a place where dead people are *buried*

clipboard (n.)
a small board. You attach paper to it, and then you can write on the paper while you are standing or moving.

clue (n.)
an object or a word that helps you to find the answer to a question

coffin (n.)
a long box for a dead body

crash (v.)
Two objects *crash* when they hit each other. If a plane *crashes*, it hits something or falls to the ground.

dig up (phr. v.)
to take out of the ground something that was *buried*

doorbell (n.)
When you arrive at a person's house, you push the *doorbell* near the door. It makes a sound like a bell in the house.

doorknob (n.)
You hold and turn a *doorknob* to open or close a door.

drawer (n.)
part of a piece of furniture. You pull it to open it, and push it to close it. You keep things in *drawers*.

drum set (n.)
You play a drum by hitting it with two sticks (= long pieces of wood), usually while other people are playing music. A *drum set* is several drums.

firefighter (n.)
a person whose job is to stop fires and save people from buildings that are burning

firework (n.)
When you burn them, *fireworks* make a loud noise, and then make many beautiful colors in the night sky.

flashlight (n.)
a small light that you carry when it is dark

forever (adv.)
for all time in the future

funeral (n.)
when people come together at a church to *bury* a dead person

hearing aid (n.)
People who cannot hear very well sometimes attach a *hearing aid* to their ear to help them to hear better.

helicopter (n.)
A *helicopter* is like a very small plane with long thin metal parts on top of it. They turn very fast to lift it into the air.

hook (n.)
a long piece of metal with a round end that you use for catching or pulling something

hug (n. and v.)
If you *hug* someone, you put your arms around them to show that you love them or like them a lot. This is a *hug*.

incredibly (adv.)
very or extremely

invent (v.); **invention** (n.)
If you *invent* something, you think of a new thing that no one has ever made before and make it. An *invention* is a new thing that no one has ever made before.

jewelry (n.)
A ring, a bracelet, and a necklace are all examples of *jewelry*.

joke (n.)
in this story, when you make someone believe something that is not true for fun

kettle (n.)
a closed pot that you use for making water boil

limousine (n.)
a very long expensive car

lonely (adj.)
You feel *lonely* when you are sad because you are alone or because you have no friends.

make sense (phr.)
If something *makes sense*, you understand it.

marriage (n.)
After their wedding, people are in a *marriage*. They have promised to love each other and stay together for all of their life.

memory (n.)
something that you remember
from the past

mission (n.)
an important idea, job or piece
of work that someone has to
make happen. It has usually
been very well planned.

neighborhood (n.)
the area that you live in

over (adv.)
finished. In this story, *over* is
used in a radio conversation to
show that the person has finished
speaking.

panic (v.); **panicky** (adj.)
to have a sudden strong feeling
of worry that stops you from
thinking clearly or deciding
what to do. *Panicky* is when
you feel *panic*.

parachute (n.)
When people jump out of a
plane, they use a *parachute*, which
suddenly opens and makes them
fall more slowly.

plug (something) in (phr. v.)
to attach a machine to a plug
(= an object that attaches to
a wall) when it stops working.
When your phone stops working,
you have to *plug it in* to make it
work again.

record (n.)
information that is kept about
people and things

remind (v.)
If someone *reminds* you of
someone, they make you think
of that person.

renter (n.)
someone who pays to live in a
house with the person who
owns it

roller coaster (n.)
a small train that goes very
high and then suddenly very
low for fun

rug (n.)
a thick, soft cover for part of
a floor

rule (n.)
something that you must or
must not do

sadness (n.)
what you feel when you are *lonely*
or when someone has died

safe-deposit box (n.)
a strong box in a bank for
important documents and money

scrapbook (n.)
a book that you keep important
pictures, letters, or newspaper
stories in

shelf (n.)
a flat piece of wood that is attached to a wall. People often put books on a *shelf*.

shovel (n.)
You use a *shovel* to lift and move snow or earth.

shrug (v.)
to move your shoulders up and then down to show that you do not know something or that you do not care very much

silence (n.)
when there are no sounds or noise at all

skyscraper (n.)
a very tall building. There are many *skyscrapers* in New York.

spotlight (n.)
a very strong light that you can point at one small area

spout (n.)
a part on a *kettle* that you pour water out of

suitcase (n.)
a large box or bag that you put your clothes in when you travel

tablecloth (n.)
You cover a table with a *tablecloth* before you eat.

tambourine (n.)
You play a *tambourine* by hitting it and shaking it, often while people are singing or playing music.

tattoo (v. and n.)
to mark a person's body with a *tattoo* (= words or pictures that stay there *forever*)

tattoo parlor (n.)
a place where you can go to have a *tattoo* drawn on your body

tear (n.)
a small amount of water that runs down your face when you cry

upset (adj. and v.)
sad or worried about something that has happened. If something makes you sad, it *upsets* you.

vase (n.)
You put flowers in a *vase* on a table or a *shelf*, for example.

walkie-talkie (n.)
a small radio that you carry, and that is like a telephone. You use it for talking to one person, or lots of people at the same time, who also have one.

wheelchair (n.)
a chair on wheels. People who are not able to walk easily use a *wheelchair* to move around.